Wisdom behind closed doors

Martina Pinto

First Published in 2021

Becomeshakespeare.com

One Point Six Technologies Pvt Ltd
123, Building J2, Shram Seva Premises,
Wadala Truck Depot,
Wadala (East), Mumbai 400037, India
T: +91 8080226699

ISBN - 978-93-5458-617-0

Preface

I am immensely grateful that you choose to read this book. It is a compilation of simple stories against the backdrop of the Covid 19 outbreak in India. I hope that these stories bring you peace, healing and assure you that you are never alone on your journey through life.

While you may have to confront various challenges, I would like to remind you that the Universe always has your back and all you need to do is believe.

Remember, life's greatest lessons reveal themselves during a crisis and the best action one could possibly take, would be to keep going with optimism, and transformation is bound to happen. I know this, as I have experienced extremely challenging times in my life, and I remember telling myself that all I need to do is make it to that finish line.

I began to write this book during the Covid 19 pandemic when I began to witness the immense strength of the human spirit amid great adversity. It felt like no matter where you came from, or who you are, each one of us is capable of reaching out and healing each other either through service or through kindness.

Before writing this book, I had several questions in my mind. The first being, if I would be able to dedicate time towards completing this book along with my commitment to work and home responsibilities, second, would my words continue to flow despite the ongoing situation around and third, would I be able to simplify life's greatest mysteries, while ensuring I stay true to my inner calling. However, I had learned early in life that hurdles are bound to come your way, your power lies in jumping over them. So, I did, and here is the book.

I hope through these simple stories you recognize the pure soul that you are and the immense strength you possess to own your happiness and your destiny.

Sending you love and light.

*Keep moving through the darkness, in time you will
be the one to bring the light*

Contents

THE DOOR

When the Door closes, on either side lie two worlds. One is a place we recognise, and the other is the one we are yet to discover. The universe works in mysterious ways, and we are drawn to places that appear ordinary at first; only to discover within them a whole new world.

From the time Madeline woke up to the sound of the alarm clock to the time she rushed out for work, she was a whirl of activity. Starting with the loud doorbell announcing the plop of the newspaper on the door mat, followed by the arrival of the milkman, she flew from task to task, before leaving the house to fight the crowds on the streets of the fast-paced city of Mumbai. She dodged the street side vendors, the vehicles and the other pedestrians and sprinted into the railway station to squeeze her way into a packed compartment in a crowded train. Only then, being held upright by her fellow passengers in a jam-packed space where she couldn't move an inch, would she relax her shoulders and draw a deep breath as she swayed with the motion of the train.

Now Madeline's world had suddenly gone quiet. She did not set the alarm each night. The doorbell did not ring anymore. Roads were deserted, shops shut, travel restricted, and there was an unsettling calm. Madeline had been restricted to the house for a week, and she was beginning to feel anxious. She used to love to travel and now even the weekends loomed empty ahead of her.

Madeline looked at the main Door and sighed, "You used to swing wide open but now you have locked us all in. Don't you feel like opening up and letting the wind in?"

 "Now is not the time."

Madeline jumped up in alarm. Who was that? Had the Door spoken to her? In a trembling voice, she asked, "You can speak?"

The Door replied, "It is only polite to reply when one is asked a question."

Madeline still couldn't believe that the Door could speak. She remained silent.

The Door said, "You need not worry, I am a friend. You can trust me."

Madeline protested, "How is it possible for a Door to speak to me?"

The Door replied, "There are many secrets in the world to discover, and sometimes their journey begins right where you are."

Madeline was on the couch. The world was closed. What could she discover from the couch? What journey could she take from the couch? She ignored the Door.

But as the days passed by, she began to look at the Door with curiosity. The Door had an imposing facade. It was made of mahogany wood with beautiful carvings. It had an ornate handle. It was set in a wall of rustic stone tiles, as if the wood and the stones came from the same period in history and carried secrets with it. The Door had been there for years. What made it speak now? It scared her.

Finally, she gathered strength and asked the Door, "While I know, I was the one to speak first, why is it after so many years you speak now?"

The Door replied, "Things are about to change drastically. It is always good to have a friend around."

Madeline smiled and somewhere within her, she was not scared anymore. She asked the Door, "When is the right time for you to open?"

The Door responded, "Why do you want me to open?"

"I want to go out..." replied Madeline.

"What's wrong in being inside?" asked the Door.

Madeline grumbled, "Well, there is nothing to do."

"There are many things you can do. Maybe it's now time to take a journey within," suggested the Door.

"What's there to journey within four rooms?" questioned Madeline.

"That's for you to discover, my dear. Some doors also open from within, you see," answered the Door.

"How do I open doors from within?" asked Madeline.

"By digging," said the Door.

Madeline was surprised. She asked, "What do you want me to dig?"

"Dig a tunnel that will lead you to a treasure that captures light and time…," said the Door.

"Do you have any leads, O Wise Door?" chuckled Madeline.

"You can begin by looking for signs," replied the Door, "while I sleep."

THE DIG

Madeline lived in an apartment on the second floor of a six-story building in the western suburbs of Mumbai in India. Whenever she thought about digging, she thought of the beach on the other side of the closed Door. How was she supposed to dig in a high-rise building? Where was she supposed to dig?

Why was she talking and listening to a Door? This isolation was playing tricks on her mind. She paced to and fro and finally entered her father's extensive library. To divert her mind, she picked up an old novel and began to read it. Soon she was engrossed in the novel.

When she flipped to page ninety-seven, a photograph slipped through the pages and landed on the floor.

She bent down to pick it up, and when she turned it over it was a photograph of herself, playing

Ludo with her father. It was from an era when life was simple and all she cared for was playtime. She used to wait the entire day for her father to return home, just to snatch away few hours of his time. There were moments when she prayed innocently to God to give her days at a stretch where she could spend time with her father. And here it was, with her father in the next room and a Door that refused to open.

She placed the photograph as a bookmark on page ninety-seven and went to a cupboard that she rarely opened to search for the Ludo game. In the cupboard she found old family photographs, handicrafts, drawings that she had long forgotten.

She stood in front of the cupboard and looked at all the old photographs. How much time had slipped through her hands yet they were captured in moments of happiness.

On the third shelf, in the corner below the box of shells, she found the Ludo Board and the dice. Filled with joy, she pulled out the board in a hurry. The box of shells fell and scattered all over the floor. The noise brought her father to the room. On seeing everything out from the cupboard, he said, "You have dug up a lot of memories, young lady."

Dug up. For a moment time stood still. She smiled at her father as if he had said the magic words.

Holding the Ludo game in her hand, she went to the closed Door. The Door said, "You have dug a lot!"

Madeline was overjoyed.

The Door continued, "In life whatever you seek, is seeking you. Whatever you ask will always be given to you. That's why I said when the time is right, I will let you out, my dear. Now don't waste time. Run along and play Ludo with your father."

Madeline smiled and said, "But what about the closed Door?"

The Door replied, "You just walked into a new one."

"Which new door?" asked Madeline.

"The Door you once prayed for."

Madeline called out to her father, "Daddy, can we play Ludo?"

His voice came back, "I love to win, get that Ludo board in."

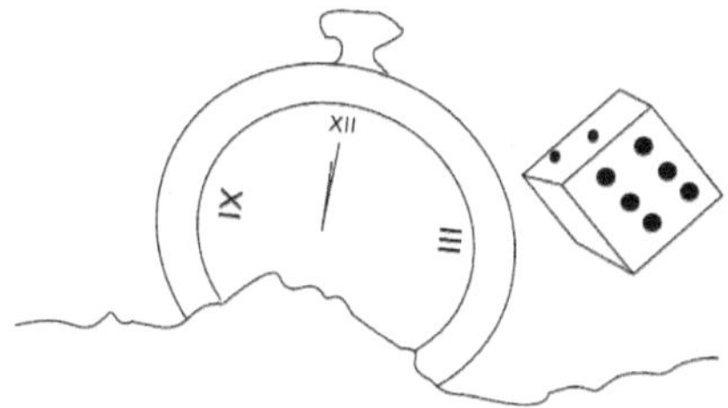

WORK FROM HOME MUSINGS

For Madeline weekends were like ice creams. Never enough even if you got a double scoop. She hurried with her Monday morning chores. However, just as she was getting ready, she remembered that the stubborn Door wouldn't let her out.

She walked casually to the Door and said, "You won't let me out today as well, will you?" Before the Door could reply, her phone rang.

The call was from her colleague who requested her to send a presentation right away. Standing beside the Door she complained, "Everybody wants everything in a hurry."

The Door began to giggle.

"What did you find so funny?" asked Madeline.

The Door replied, "It is funny how you lose your cool and begin to complain."

Madeline replied angrily, "You would have done the same."

The Door said, "Every action has its consequences, Madeline. Remember it's never the situation, it's always your response to it. That's what makes the real difference."

After ten minutes, her colleague called again, "How long will it take? I need to send it as soon as possible. The client called again."

Madeline glanced at the Door and replied, "Just doing a final check." She began to meticulously go through the presentation and when it seemed fine, she emailed it.

Soon after, Pia, who was Madeline's go-to person at work, called to check on how she was doing. Half an hour into the conversation, Pia said, "You know what? I heard that for the next two months we can't take any time off."

"You can't be serious! How can they do this to us?" said Madeline.

Pia added, "You never know what's coming your way next."

A call that would have made Madeline feel good, had instead left her in a bad mood. Madeline hung up and began to grumble, "Now we can't even take leave?"

The Door asked calmly, "Are you sure?"

"Well, if Pia told me, it should be true. Now I have to wait for them to make it official," replied Madeline.

The Door said, "Don't cross bridges till you come to them."

In the days that followed, Madeline seemed annoyed and snappy. The Door tried to make a conversation, but she seemed to be too busy caught up with the voices in her head.

The Door found it hard to see her so agitated so it gathered the courage and asked her, "Can you get for me a bucket of water?"

Madeline ignored the request at first, but when the Door asked her again, she obliged.

"Where do you want me to keep it?" asked Madeline.

The Door said, "I want you to hold it in your hand as long as you can."

"What kind of joke is this?" asked an annoyed Madeline.

The Door said, "I want to see how strong you are."

Madeline decided that it was time to teach the Door a lesson, so she held on to the bucket.

The Door smiled.

After five minutes her hands began to ache, but she continued to hold on to the bucket, just to show the Door how strong she was. It was now almost half an hour and she was finding it hard to hold the bucket. Slowly with much hesitation she lowered it to the ground. She rubbed her hands together to relieve the pain and numbness.

The Door said, "Your hands are in pain."

"Yes, because of you," said Madeline.

Softly the Door said, "I only told you to hold it in your hands for as long as you could, but in your rage, you stood with it for half an hour. You held on to it so tightly that it began to hurt you. My dear, the more you hold on to anything, be it anger, opinions or rumours it will harm you and leave you numb. What Pia told you could have been just a rumour, but you have been holding on to it for a week now. You have been getting irritated and having sleepless nights. It's time you know for how long you should carry a load."

Madeline's phone rang. The Door was right. It was Pia informing Madeline that it was all just a rumour and that they could apply for leave. Madeline breathed a sigh of relief and understood what the Door meant. She looked at the Door and smiled.

The Door replied, "Let it all go. Nothing is worth your peace."

SOULFUL CARVINGS

Alive within us is a part that sees the world differently. That demolishes all prejudices and boundaries and walks out the Door into freedom. Where there is no question of right or wrong, just creative expression and woven emotions. Painting gave Madeline this freedom.

It was a Saturday afternoon, and the Door was still adamant about not letting her out, so she decided to paint.

Madeline took out a canvas and began to sketch rough lines on it. She then took out her paints and, dipping her brush into a bottle of rustic brown colour, delicately moved the brush onto the canvas. Her face lit up with every stroke of paint. The Door had never seen her as much at peace as she was at this moment.

She let the sap green trickle down her brush onto the canvas and then she ran the brush on the canvas like a feather being blown by the breeze. After she painted the background, she let the paint dry. As she sat there staring at it, her thoughts began to drift. Suddenly she raised her head and said to the Door, "When will it be the right time for you to open?"

"You will know," replied the Door.

"How would I know?" said Madeline.

The Door smiled and said, "Within you lie the keys of time, love, and purpose that open closed doors."

Madeline began to nod in comprehension. By then the paint on the canvas had dried up. Madeline began to paint again. She let her brush draw the arch followed by the lines that connected the arch.

The Door exclaimed, "That looks like a painting of me!"

"Yes, it is you. What do you think?"

"I think we are going to get better with each passing day," said the Door.

Madeline looked at the painting, and added some finishing touches and said, "I may have found a vocation there."

The Door laughed and said, "Breathe and keep moving."

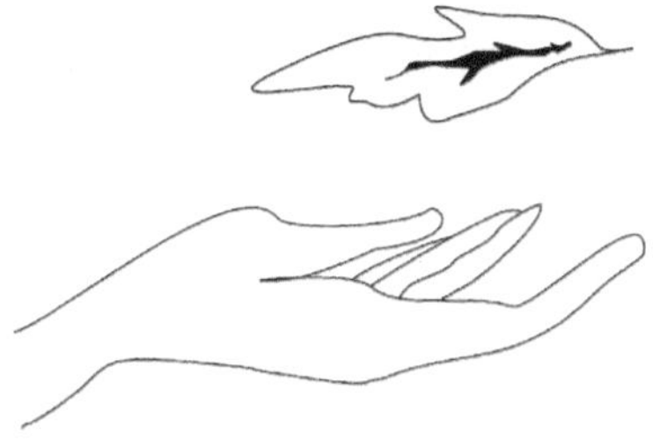

PAW PRINTS

The moment you hold them in your hand and call them your own is the very moment they hold you in their heart forever. Such is their unconditional love that they fill the emptiness within us, something we never knew existed.

Madeline was busy working when suddenly, from behind the open laptop, popped up two little eyes with furry ears and a wet nose. It was Toby, a long-haired dachshund. Madeline had welcomed him in her home three years ago, and ever since they were like two peas in a pod.

On seeing Toby look at her with his playful puppy eyes, she knew he wanted to play with her. On most days when Madeline was at home, she and Toby would play fetch inside the building compound. Now, with the Door not letting them out, Madeline decided to play with Toby at home. Toby didn't mind at all. As long as Madeline and he were spending time together, the rest didn't matter.

Toby loved to play tug of war, so Madeline took out the cotton rope and played with him. She followed it with a game of hide-and-seek. When both of them had tired themselves out, they sat under the fan. She looked at the Door and said, "This little guy here saved my life."

The Door asked in surprise, "How?"

Madeline said, "There was a time in my life when I had lost all direction and I didn't know where my life was heading. I tried to keep afloat but the pain within held on to me like a giant claw. I could see myself sinking. And then Toby came along... he was hardly bigger than the size of my palm. As I picked him up, he began to chew on my fingers, and soon dozed off to sleep. I was then a stranger to him but the trust he had in me, made me hold on to him. I wonder that day, who held on to whom..." She ran her hand over Toby's head.

Toby cuddled closer to her.

The Door, who witnessed the bond between them, said, "Maybe, sometimes when you save others, you end up saving yourself."

NEW LIFE

They always grow towards the light, each knowing their purpose, each revealing the magic of creation, and spreading cheer to those around them with bountiful flowers and fruits.

Madeline was very fond of plants and had ten potted plants sitting on the windowsill. Ever since the Door refused to open, she sat beside the window and watch the plants sway in the cool summer breeze. She considered that part of her home to be her private little garden. All her plants were very dear to her, and she even renamed some of them when she felt their original names did not do justice to how magnificent they looked. She watered her plants every morning.

One day she noticed her double flowering Crape Jasmine plant had begun to shed leaves. At first, she thought that the shedding of a few leaves wouldn't matter, but to her astonishment, within a week the plant stood there bare of all its leaves.

What was going wrong? Was it just the season or had the plant attracted any pests that killed it? Nevertheless, she kept watering the plant along with the others. After a week she began to worry as the Jasmine plant didn't bear any new leaves. Whenever she looked at the bare plant, a small part within her wished for it to bloom again.

Seeing her upset, the Door said, "I see you have been upset for quite a while now."

Madeline replied, "It's my plant! It's been weeks now and I've seen no new leaves. I don't want to let my plant go."

The Door replied, "Tell me what you want the plant to do?"

Madeline burst out, "I want the plant to be healthy with green leaves and white flowers like before."

At the outburst, the Door said calmly, "Imagine the reality you want, not the reality that is."

"What do you mean?" asked Madeline.

The Door explained, "We live in a world of endless possibilities, and you should always imagine what you want, no matter what the reality appears to be. If you want leaves and flowers to bloom, imagine it being that way. Also, talk to the Jasmine plant about how beautiful its flowers are, how you love its frills. The universe is alive, Madeline, all you need to do is share your aspirations with it."

Madeline listened attentively and said, "What if none of this is true?"

The Door replied, "At least you gave it a try…"

So, the next day Madeline began to see the plant like it used to be, packed with luscious green leaves and pretty white flowers with frills. She told the plant how happy she was to see its flowers. Suddenly one morning, while she was watering the plants like she always did, she saw a little green shoot. She couldn't believe it at first, but then in a day or two, it grew into a leaf. She was overjoyed and ran to the Door exclaiming, "It's working!! The plant has grown a new leaf. This is simply amazing. I am going to rename this plant."

"What would you call it?" the Door asked.

Looking lovingly at the plant, Madeline replied, "New Life."

PIECE OF THE SKY

When you feel there is nowhere to go, look up at the sky, and you will find your space in an infinite galaxy. Behind the cotton clouds and the boundless sky, let your imagination drift away to a place of serenity and calm.

While the Door continued to stay closed, Madeline woke up early, before sunrise, and watched the earth light up. She heard the chirping of birds and observed how nature woke up to the rising of the sun.

This morning, as she looked up at the sky, a soft morning breeze brushed across her face, and it felt like the earth had blown her a kiss. Looking at the Door she said, "It's a wonderful morning, isn't it?"

The Door responded, "It truly is!"

Madeline then continued with her household chores and got ready for work. Over the months it had become a habit to look at the sky before she began her work. This helped clear her mind and allowed fresh ideas to flow in.

That day, Madeline was deeply engrossed in her work, and she didn't realise when it was noon. Suddenly the day grew dull as grey clouds began to roll across the sky. This distracted her and she went to the window to look out. Her brother came to her room and told her the weather report had predicted a storm. This always meant a power failure.

She rushed to the laptop to see if the battery was charged. She looked at the sky and said, "You seemed so bright and sunny this morning and now it seems like you may just burst into a downpour any time."

An unsettling silence that seemed to have filled the room.

"What will we do?" exclaimed Madeline.

The Door replied, "Keep your gaze towards the sky."

"I see no birds flying," said Madeline.

"The universe whispers to each one of us. We are all connected. In silence, we all speak the same language, and in silence we all understand," replied the Door.

Madeline nodded as she saw the sky get dense with clouds. After a roll of thunder, down came the rain, ferocious, lashing out at the earth.

Madeline exclaimed, "It seems like it is here to cause destruction!!"

The Door said, "The storm always feels like it has the power to destroy everything in its path, but it fails to realise that it is only scattering itself and at one point it will be empty."

It poured for nearly two hours and then in the distance appeared a beautiful beam of light. Madeline pointed towards the light said, "Look at that ray of golden light. Seems like the sun is smiling from behind the clouds. The birds are flying back to their nests. I wish I could go out to experience all of it."

The Door knew what Madeline was hinting at and said, "You already did."

Madeline smiled and said, "Do you have an answer for everything?"

the door replied, "only for the ones you seek"

JUST COOK IT

We are no different from the Earth. We carry its energy within us when we feed on its fruits and grains.

Madeline loved to try out different cuisines and was used to ordering food from restaurants. She preferred not to carry lunch from home. All her life, she had heard her relatives say, girls need to know how to cook. It was this expectation and her rebellious nature, which made sure she never learnt to cook.

As the Door wouldn't open, Madeline couldn't order food from a restaurant. There were days when she wished she could order in from her favourite restaurant.

Then one Saturday evening, while looking out of the window she thought of days she used to travel, to explore new places. Looking at her pet dog Toby, she said, "If only we could go out! We would be by the sea right now. How I miss the sound of the waves and the *anda bhurji*." Toby looked at her with tender eyes that revealed he felt the same.

The Door said, "Do you know what is as good as travelling? Savouring the food of the land."

Madeline looked at him and asked, "Are you suggesting that I cook?" She sat up straight and was ready for a heated conversation.

The Door replied, "I thought you love to explore…"

"I do, but what has that got to do with me wanting to cook? I have never liked cooking. Is that what all women are supposed to do?" asked Madeline crossly.

The Door knew that this was coming from a place that needed healing. Sometimes the words people say stay with us and keep hurting. The Door said, "I want you to explore the world on your platter for which all you need is the right ingredients, and you will get to taste the food of the land. So tell me, Madeline, what would you like to have?"

"Well, I would love to have a *nda bhurji* for now," giggled Madeline.

The Door said, "Why don't you Google some videos on YouTube that will teach you how to prepare it? Don't worry, it's just your family and me that's around. I won't let anyone in. So, go ahead. No one is even watching."

Madeline clicked on the YouTube icon on her phone. She typed 'Anda Bhurji recipe' and several video links came up in the search. Madeline scrolled through and clicked on the video whose thumbnail was appetizing.

She entered the kitchen and took two eggs from the refrigerator. Next, she chopped the onions and tomatoes. Once she had all the ingredients ready, she looked at Toby and said, "Here I go!" She tossed the onions into the frying pan, then added the tomatoes and the spices just as the YouTube video had instructed. After a quick stir, in went the eggs.

The Door reminded, "Don't forget the salt."

She smiled and added the salt. Looking at the *anda bhurji*, Madeline's face lit up. Cooking was not such a bad idea after all.

The Door sniffed and said, "It looks delicious to me."

Madeline sat at the table by the window, took her first mouthful and exclaimed, "I am good at this!!" Madeline relished what she had cooked and gave a little to Toby, who gobbled it up happily. "I had it wrong all these years. Today I realised it was not the cooking that I disliked, but expectations of women cooking that made me hate cooking."

The Door said, "Never mind, just be glad you realised it."

FESTIVE SPIRIT

Festivals exist to bear witness to a time of triumph when light appeared amidst darkness. A light that is carried through generations to remind the world of hope and love that surrounds us.

It was September and the festive season was approaching. Madeline was anxious and gloomy. "It won't be the same this time," she grumbled. "We can't visit anyone, neither can anyone visit us. You remember, last year Ritu Aunty brought us *besan ladoos* for Diwali, which was simply delicious. Just thinking of them makes my mouth water."

Looking at the gloom on Madeline's face her mother said, "Don't worry. This year we will try making *besan ladoos* at home. Your brother can help us, too. Won't you, Chris?"

Chris was busy dunking biscuit in his tea and on hearing this he exclaimed, "What? Don't expect any help from me!"

His mother gave him a determined look that said *you don't have a choice*. He looked at Madeline angrily, but she was enjoying what was going on.

The thought of festivals not being celebrated the way they used to troubled Madeline. "How will it be Diwali without fireworks, presents, or friends exchanging sweets? How will it be Christmas without midnight mass and a Christmas party?" she said looking at the Door.

The Door then said let me narrate a story of a village in Siena, of a time when wars were still fought with swords and spears.

The land was at war for nearly a year. People hid in cellars and there was barely enough food to last for a month. To make matters worse it was December, and the cold was at its peak. The villagers were nervous and tense. Christmas was soon approaching but there was nothing to celebrate in a war.

Living in the cellar was a little girl named Anne and her two-year-old sister and mother. On Christmas Eve, Anne's mother narrated the Christmas Story to both her daughters as she tucked them into bed.

Anne looked all around with deep sadness. She got up from her bed. Her mother was busy putting her younger sister to sleep. Anne walked to the centre of the cellar and began to sing, "Hark the herald angels sing." One by one, the other people in the cellar began to sing along with her. No one cared about the dangers of being discovered by the enemy. The Christmas spirit had found its way into their hearts... In those moments they experienced pure love, peace, and bliss.

An old man walked up to little Anne and asked, "What made you sing, little girl?"

"Christmas!" she replied.

The Door continued, "You see, Madeline, the festive spirit always finds its way into our soul. It is not bound by people, sweets, or customs. Our hearts connect to the positive energy that surrounds us."

Madeline nodded, "That's true! We will be celebrating Diwali soon. Mom was right. We should try making *besan ladoos* ourselves. I will also light some *diyas* and place them on the window."

The Door replied, "That would be wonderful!"

"I just don't know what gifts to give everyone..." wondered Madeline.

The Door replied, "Just be the spirit that spreads light and happiness."

FEATHER TWEETS

They rise with the sun and with their melodious voice they wake up the world. Listen, as they bring messages, from the Universe, of peace and freedom that nourishes the spirit.

Madeline loved to water her plants every morning. The way her plants would sway as the water trickled down to the bottom of the pots, and the earthly scent that rose from the soil brought her a great sense of healing. One day, a sparrow flew to her window and began to drink the water that surfaced on top of the soil in the pots. Madeline was delighted. She exclaimed, "Did you see that? The little sparrow drank water from that pot. I wish it would come every day."

The Door was happy that Madeline was finding happiness in little things. It said, "Yes, it's indeed wonderful. If you want the sparrow to come again, keep a bowl full of water near the window.

Hunger and thirst are felt by all. Share with the Universe what you can."

Madeline went into the kitchen and filled a bowl with water and placed it by the window, hoping the sparrow would visit her soon. however, to her disappointment, it didn't turn up the next day or the day after. She changed the water every day but there was no sign of the sparrow. Finally, one day when she couldn't wait anymore, she looked at the Door and said, "I'm not keeping the bowl full of water anymore. Not a single bird comes to drink from it."

The Door smiled and said, "You don't need to do that. Just close your eyes, take a deep breath, and talk to the birds through your thoughts. Tell them you have placed a bowl of water outside for them. Don't force them to visit, just let them know that they are always welcome."

Madeline did exactly what the Door advised her to do. The very next day she saw the sparrow sipping water from the bowl. Her joy knew no bounds. She was delighted.

Many other birds began to visit and became frequent visitors.

Madeline grew curious and wondered how it all came together. Just then the little sparrow arrived.

Madeline whispered, "How did you know I was calling you?"

The little bird looked at Madeline and said, "When anyone welcomes us in their hearts, we visit them in their homes."

FULL MOON

The night began to cast its spell. Looking up at the dark sky through her window Madeline thought of days when she would travel to faraway lands and lie on the ground to watch the stars along with her friends. The nights were now being spent behind locked Doors in uncertainty.

That night the crescent moon was smiling through the scattered clouds. Madeline looked up at the moon and the solitude she felt in her heart mingled with that of the moon. She said, "Doesn't the moon fear the darkness?"

The Door said: He once did but not anymore. The moon was once a playful little child. He would wander the galaxies to experience its wonders. Till the day came when he had to fulfil his purpose - which was to watch the night sky for Earth. He was not ready, yet he had to take up the role because the laws of the Universe couldn't be disobeyed.

On his first day, as he was dropped into darkness, he grew cold with fear and stood silently in the dark. The Universe watched his struggle but kept calm. The Earth looking at the Moon said, "You are no good, you can't even shine…" The moon heard the harsh words and said to himself, "Why did the Universe have to put me here if I was no good?" That night the moon stayed in the sky with no light.

Then one day he happened to look down at the Earth, he saw a few travellers who were lost in the dark. He wanted to help them, so he gathered the strength and peeped out of the darkness. Seeing the light, the travellers thanked him. But the waters on the earth roared. The moon was unable to understand why the waters were so furious on seeing him venture out from the dark.

Firmly, he held on to his decision to be the light for travellers in the dark. He put his fears behind him and began to show himself a little more each day in the dark sky. The stars were inspired and decided to join him. One day, he was whole. He shone brilliantly in the dark. The Earth said, "You look so beautiful, how did you do it?" The moon replied, "I had to let go of things that weighed me down; the darkness, the furious waters, and above all my own fear. Watching those travellers walk in my light gave me immense happiness and the strength to keep going. It became my purpose and after that nothing else mattered."

Madeline kept her gaze on the moon that seemed to be smiling at her. She said, "So it was the travellers who made the moon shine so bright?"

The Door smiled and said, "I wouldn't say that. I feel sometimes we find ourselves while trying to help others."

HEROES WITHOUT CAPES

Behind doors that refuse to open lies a dark world where heroes fight battles we know nothing about. We think we are bound within walls, but the ones in the open long for the warmth and comfort of the four walls of their home.

The Door always told Madeline that it would open when the time was right. Weeks turned into months and the Door stayed closed. Madeline could hear the frequent sound of the ambulances from the other side of the Door. "What do you see on the other side?" she asked the Door.

The Door replied, "It's something I wanted to hide from you. But I guess it's time to tell you what's outside. There is silence in chaos. People have covered their faces to protect themselves, but their eyes speak of fear. They say an invisible slayer walks free, whose appetite grows when it sees people gather. So now I see very few people out of their homes and not more than two together."

The Door saw the fear in Madeline's eyes and said, "While what I have told you may seem very frightening, but every day I also see superheroes."

"Superheroes!" exclaimed Madeline.

"Yes," said the Door. "They have lived in the shadows for all these years. Now they are recognised for their invaluable service to mankind. They don't look like the imaginary ones we know of. They don't wear capes or fancy outfits. They are ordinary beings and I wonder what gives them the willpower and courage, to leave their families behind and walk through the door every day to save lives."

Madeline said, "Maybe they are warriors of a different kind."

The Door said, "Yes, they are."

Madeline asked, "Why is the slayer doing this, what will it get from all of this?"

The Door replied, "Just like every superhero doesn't wear a cape, not every slayer comes with the purpose to destroy. Some come to create."

"How can a slayer ever create?" asked Madeline

The Door replied, "Everything in this Universe is put in its place with a purpose. The slayer is here to destroy, so that it can make way for the new."

"The world was perfect…" said Madeline.

"Yes, it was, but people forgot that the world was not just theirs. The world belongs to trees, animals, birds, fishes as well as the tiniest of insects. It belongs to the rivers, mountains, and seas. Remember what I told you, Madeline - the Universe is alive. Listening, watching, and hearing everything. Yes, the world was perfect for you; not for others who also share this world with you."

"What will it take to send the slayer back to where it came from?" asked Madeline.

"A change of heart," replied the Door.

"Will that scare away the slayer?" asked Madeline.

"No, it will know that its work is done," said the Door.

"Then why isn't anyone changing their ways?" exclaimed Madeline.

The Door said, "My dear, that's where the real battle is being fought. That's where the slayer arrives. The trick is to change your ways before it does."

"How do we know what to change?" asked Madeline.

The Door replied, "You can begin by can asking yourself three questions. Have I been true to myself? Have I loved unconditionally? Have I made a difference to the world around me through acts of kindness?"

BONDS OF FRIENDSHIP

They are souls who have travelled through capsules of time, to catch your sunshine smile and to be with you when the world around goes wild. Distance and time don't matter, because the soul knows you will always find each other.

Madeline had many close friends while growing up, but time led them to walk on different paths. Some were driven by ambition, others by responsibility, while some stepped into a new family. While they all cherished each memory of the times spent with one another, they could now never find time to meet. Among them were some relationships which were strained with no one taking the initiative to fix them.

Now, when Madeline was locked within the four walls of the house, she had time to look back at the days gone by. She thought of her friends and remembered the times when they would gather and talk about everything under the sun till the wee hours. Thinking of those days made her smile. She recalled how mischievous she was when she was younger and remembering her reaction to certain situations in those days, made her smile sheepishly.

"I never realised I was creating memories," said Madeline as she scrolled through the pictures on her phone. "I wish I had met my friends more often and made an effort to stay connected. I just kept running and today when I sit in silence, it's not those long working hours, meetings or presentations that I think of. Rather it's those moments I spent with my friends which fill me with happiness." She turned to the Door and said, "Do my friends feel the same way? Do they think of me like I think of them?"

"We never forget anyone who enters our life, Madeline. Good or bad they stay alive in our memories. Why don't you give them a call if you miss them so much?" suggested the Door.

"Things are different now and above all it's been years since I last spoke to any of them. Also, I don't have a reason to call them," sighed Madeline.

The Door said, "You don't need a reason to call your friends. You just need to dial and say hello. Why don't you try calling someone right away? I see you have the numbers. How about you start by calling Advika?"

Madeline said, "Well, not her for the first call. Let me see." She began to scroll through numbers on her phone and said, "Let me try calling Isha. Here I go."

A conversation that Madeline had expected would end in five minutes took up an entire hour. She hung up the phone and said, "Felt so good talking to her after years. Nothing seems to have changed. Looks like I imagine things in my head that is not true."

"If that made you feel good, you should call your other friends too," said the Door.

Madeline agreed, and one by one she dialled each of her friends who were once close to her. Every call seemed to have its uniqueness, be it the memories or the jokes which no one else knew about. Her face brightened, and her soul was at peace.

Then the Door asked, "Did you call Advika?"

Miffed, Madeline looked at the Door and asked, "Why do you want me to call Advika? I don't talk to her anymore - we didn't part ways on good terms. We had a huge fight and it's never been the same."

"Well, that makes it even more important for you to speak to her. What are you waiting for?" asked the Door.

"I can't. It's too messed up, and why do you keep insisting that I call her? She doesn't remember me nor does she bother to apologise. Why should I? Anyway I am extremely happy to have spoken to many of my friends. Just let me be," urged Madeline.

The Door left the matter alone.

The next day, when Madeline was sipping her morning tea, the Door said, "You are set free by love. Those you hold a grudge against will never leave you. With them, you have imprisoned yourself. Not just for a lifetime, but eternity."

Madeline was startled. She said, "Is this regarding Advika?"

The Door replied, "No, this is regarding you. I don't want you to be a captive."

"Captive of whom?" asked Madeline.

"Captive of your pain," replied the Door. "When you have a grudge against someone, you refuse to forgive them. So we don't forgive ourselves."

Madeline asked, "But how is it about me forgiving myself?"

"When we say we can't forgive someone, we decide not to release that pain which that person has inflicted on us. So tell me, who's holding on to the pain?" asked the Door.

Madeline stayed silent for a while, staring into space . She was trying to understand what the Door had explained to her.

The Door continued, "Let the grudge go, Madeline. If not for the other person, at least for yourself."

"She left me when I wanted her the most. I was going through such a difficult time, and all I wanted was for her to hear me out. Instead, she just shut me out."

"Free the pain, break the chains," replied the Door.

"It's not that easy…" confessed Madeline.

"Well, you can take the first step," said the Door.

"What would that be?" asked Madeline.

"Releasing the pain," replied the Door.

"And what should be the second step?" asked Madeline.

"Call Advika," replied the Door.

"What if she doesn't respond?" asked Madeline.

"At least you will be released from your pain," answered the Door.

EXODUS

When the clouds of darkness venture near and gold loses its glitter, what binds man has now released him to find his real treasure. He must return to his roots and embrace a mother who he knew was home.

Madeline got done with work early. So she decided to make pancakes for everyone at home for tea. Into the bowl went the flour, baking powder, salt, and sugar. She gave it a good mix and made the pancakes.

Her father exclaimed, "You have made them just like your grandma used to. After she left us, I thought I would never be able to enjoy the taste of pancakes again."

Madeline's mother rolled her eyes and said, "Why didn't you learn the recipe from her?"

Madeline and Chris began to laugh. Tea-time was always about light-hearted debates and teasing each other, but ultimately Toby would steal the show with his sparkling puppy eyes and mischievous ways.

Madeline felt contented. She said, "It's wonderful when you are locked up with your favourite people. I am sure it is the same for many out there."

The Door replied, "Unfortunately not all. For many it's about travelling back to their homes."

"What do you mean?" asked Madeline.

"Millions of people migrated to big cities to earn their livelihood. When Doors suddenly closed around the country, millions were left stranded without income or food. They were helpless, and didn't know where to go. All they could think of was the home they left behind. With no transport to get back home, they began their journey on foot. Old and young, men and women, some walked back with their children for more than 200 miles."

Madeline was shocked on hearing this. "Why are they going back?" asked Madeline.

"There is nothing left for them here. Without any income how can they survive?" replied the Door.

"How will it help if they return to their native place. Wouldn't it be the same?" asked Madeline.

The Door replied, "It won't be the same."

"Why?" asked Madeline.

"Tell me," said the Door, "whom did you go to as a child when you were hurt or hungry?"

"My mother," replied Madeline.

The Door asked, "Why did you do that?"

"Because I knew that if I was hungry, she would feed me. If I was hurt, she would be the one to wrap her arms around me, and I would feel safe," replied Madeline.

"Now you are old enough and you can look after your own needs. But on days when you are unwell, who would you like to be with, and where would you want to be?"

"I would love to be at home with mom," replied Madeline.

"So it is with each one of us. We may travel the world and earn riches but when that fades away all we want to do is return home."

Madeline asked, "Will all of them reach their homes?"

The Door gave her a cold look. "No, my dear, not all will reach home."

"Then what gives them the strength to walk that road?" asked Madeline.

The Door replied, "Love. That is calling them home."

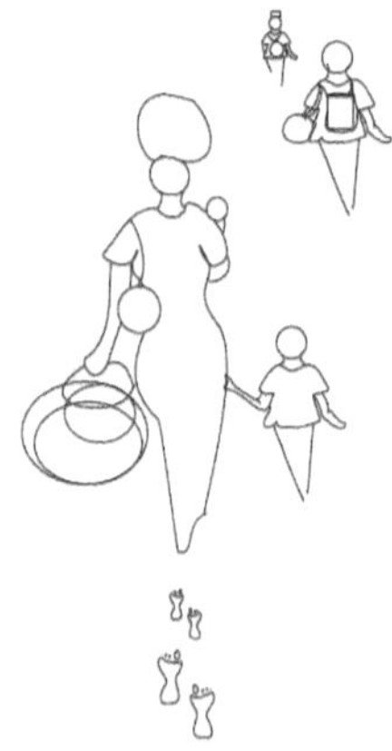

THE UNEXPECTED VISITOR

When you don't understand what's happening, trust the Universe completely. It may not reveal its plan to you at that moment, but one day you will be surprised with its purpose.

Madeline loved to watch the setting sun to view the artistry of the Universe. It was summer and the scarlet flowers of the Gulmohar tree had blossomed gracefully. So exhilarating was their beauty in the golden sunlight that the wind seemed to be waltzing with them. While she was admiring this beauty, she spotted a squirrel on the tree. She was delighted to see how the little fellow balanced on the branches of the Gulmohar tree. As if he was performing for her, the squirrel leaped and landed on her window. Madeline jumped off her seat in fright. She said, "You are brave, little one." The squirrel kept his gaze on her. She sprinted to the bedroom to get her phone to click a photograph with the squirrel. When she returned, the squirrel was gone.

The next day, the squirrel appeared again. Again, she ran to get her phone, but before she could reach the window, the squirrel was nowhere in sight. It was one mischievous squirrel! thought Madeline. The following day, Madeline kept her phone with her in case the squirrel came again. But there was no sign of him.

A few days later, one evening at sunset, the squirrel appeared again. Madeline didn't run for her phone. Instead, she looked at the squirrel and smiled. The squirrel stayed and cautiously approached her. Both of them watched the sunset. Curious, Madeline turned to the squirrel and asked, "Why do you run away every time I get my phone?"

The squirrel looked at the sun.

"I know you can understand what I am saying, so tell me why?" probed Madeline.

The squirrel kept silent.

Miffed, she looked at the squirrel and said, "Well fine, I won't say a thing."

Two huge birds flew by. They looked like cotton candy with huge wings. Within seconds they were gone.

"Wow! Did you see that?" exclaimed Madeline. "They were flamingos."

The squirrel's face lit up. "Wasn't that beautiful?" the squirrel exclaimed.

Madeline was dumbstruck. "You talk?" she exclaimed.

The squirrel replied, "Only if you choose to listen."

"Then why were you quiet all this while?" asked Madeline.

"Because we were watching the sunset," said the squirrel.

Madeline said, "Since you can talk, I have a bunch of questions."

"Shoot," replied the squirrel.

"Why do you disappear every time I get my phone?" asked Madeline.

The squirrel replied, "Some moments need to be experienced and treasured in the heart, not through photographs. These moments will stay with you no matter where you are."

She asked, "Why did you come to meet me?"

The squirrel replied, "I have seen you looking out of the window, waiting for the day when you will be allowed out into the world again."

Madeline sighed. "It is the same day after day. It is nearly six months since I have been at home. I was an avid traveller. Being in the midst of nature gave me immense peace. It cleared my mind."

The squirrel comforted her saying, "Nature always looks after her own. She knows you can't meet her the way you used to. That's why I am here."

"Mother nature has sent you to me?" exclaimed Madeline.

"Yes," replied the squirrel. "She sent you a gift, here it is."

Madeline held out her hand and the squirrel placed a few seeds on her palm. "What seeds are these?" asked Madeline.

"They are sunflower seeds," replied the squirrel.

"Do you know why Mother Nature sent me sunflower seeds?" asked a curious Madeline.

The squirrel responded, "When a seed is planted does it know that it will one day grow into a tree?"

"Maybe not," replied Madeline.

The squirrel went on. "The seed lives in darkness for nearly ten to fifteen days. The person planting the seeds knows that if the seeds are buried well in the soil they will sprout and grow into a plant. So it is with you, Madeline. Today you are within the four walls of your home. Just like the seed, remember you've only been planted and very soon it will all make sense."

The sun was now a thin line of orange on the horizon. The squirrel looked at Madeline and said, "It's time for me to leave."

"Will you visit me again?" asked Madeline.

The squirrel replied, "Yes, just keep your face to the sunshine."

SECRET TO HAPPINESS

Know that the universe chose you to live another day, for you fit into its plan so gracefully. But you will realise this only at the right time. Till then, be grateful for all that you have, and be assured that for every step you take, the universe will support you to achieve more.

Madeline thought about what the squirrel told her. She made an effort to keep herself happy in whichever way she could. She spent more time speaking to her family, engaging in hobbies, talking to friends, trying new recipes. She even made a list of her favourite movies to watch. She stuck to this practice for a week before she began to lose interest and slipped back into her old ways.

She looked at the Door and mumbled, "It's so difficult to keep yourself always happy. It needs so much effort. There is always something missing."

The Door said, "Happiness is not a destination. It is the journey."

"In that case," argued Madeline, "I will never be able to find happiness."

"That's not true," comforted the Door. "Happiness has a secret ingredient which very few know about."

"Will you share that secret ingredient with me?" asked Madeline.

The Door replied, "I surely will. First, you need to tell me what according to you brings happiness?"

Madeline thought for a while and said, "Being surrounded by family and friends, being in good health, having sufficient money to cover my needs, and pursuing my passion."

The Door said, "You have it all. Then why aren't you happy?"

"Maybe I want a little more," smirked Madeline.

The Door laughed and said, "Well, what if you were granted that little more you ask for? Would you be happy then?"

Again, Madeline thought for a while and said, "I am not sure…"

The Door continued, "Exactly! That's because the desire to have a little more will always keep you away from your happiness."

"Then is it wrong to have a desire?" asked Madeline.

The Door replied, "Desires have no boundaries, Madeline. If you place your happiness in its hands, each desire will claim a share and run, and you will not know where to look for it. So, own your happiness."

"How can one own happiness?" asked Madeline.

The Door replied, "When you are grateful for everything you have, you own your happiness. The Universe is alive. When you thank it for all that you have, it responds with much more. For it is written for him who has much, more will be given, and he will have abundance; but for him who has not, even what he has will be taken away. So always give thanks for all that you have. Now that I have revealed to you the secret, what do I get?"

Madeline looked loving at the Door and said, "Thank you."

LOOK FOR SIGNS

There is a world that we find mysterious, that our five senses tend to deny, but there are always signs to guide us. All we need to do is recognise them when they arrive.

One night while everyone was asleep, Madeline woke up from a nightmare and began shivering with fear.

She reached for her watch. It was four-thirty in the morning. As it was still dark outside, she stayed in bed waiting for the sun to rise.

As soon as the room brightened, she went into the kitchen for a drink of water. She poured water into a glass. She looked at the Door and said, "It was terrible in my dream. The sun was covered by a shadow and trees began to fall. The waters of rivers became dark and I could hear people cry in the distance. It was awful. I saw a man run towards his village crying out, it's an eclipse. The air was heavy. It was dreadful and I couldn't take it anymore. Luckily, I woke up and realised it was a dream."

The Door comforted her saying, "You are awake now. Don't be scared."

But Madeline knew something was wrong. "It seems like my dream scared you," probed Madeline as she took a sip of water.

The Door replied, "The universe sends us signs and dreams are one of them. When we sleep, we close our eyes to the physical world and open our eyes to universal consciousness and knowledge. To an enigma of revelations. That's where thoughts mirror and manifest."

"So, my dream was a sign? Not a happy one though," remarked Madeline.

"All signs are good, Madeline. They are here to guide and prepare us for the time to come," replied the Door.

"Do you know what my dream meant?" asked Madeline.

"An eclipse is always a sign of rapid change. It shadows the light and manoeuvres in the darkness to accomplish what it is set out to do. Such change often comes with a price, Madeline," explained the Door.

"What kind of price?" probed Madeline.

"A price that's irreversible, a price that you can't bargain with," answered the Door.

"So where does that leave us? Are we that powerless against change?" asked Madeline.

The Door could grasp the anxiety that was building up in Madeline's mind. "Change is inevitable, my dear. The way we respond to it can either break or transform us. Our response determines whether we choose to be powerless or fearless," replied the Door.

"Are there always signs to guide us?" asked Madeline.

"The universe is very kind to all of us. It always wants to direct us on a path that leads to our purpose here on earth. That's why we are always given signs," explained the Door.

Madeline continued, "Why does the universe use signs to communicate? Why doesn't it talk to us like you and the squirrel?"

The Door replied, "Let me tell you a story."

Once a Guru called two of his disciples - Drona and Nakul and asked them if they could fetch him two pots of water from the river. The river was nearly 150 kilometers away from where they were. The disciples agreed to go. But the way to the river was through the forest. The Guru reassured them that he would always be there to guide them. Content with his words, they set out on their journey. Both the disciples had once accompanied their Guru to the river, so they were familiar with the route. After having walked for nearly four hours, they observed animal footprints on the ground that pointed in the opposite direction from where they were heading. Nakul expressed his concern to Drona and suggested that they follow the animal footprints.

Drona was not convinced and insisted that they should carry on in the direction they were headed. But Nakul was firm. So, they decided to take different routes.

Drona kept walking and after having walked for ten kilometers, he noticed that the trees on his path were dry and withered. Nevertheless, he continued walking till he reached the banks of the river. To his anguish, the river was dry. Disheartened he returned to the ashram. When he entered the Guru's room, he saw Nakul's pot filled to the brim with water. "How is it possible?" argued Drona "I went to the river and it was dry. I don't believe this water is from the river."

The Guru assured him that it was from the river.

Drona said, "You promised that you would guide us. Why did you guide Nakul and not me?"

The Guru waited for him to calm down. He said "I can't tell you what path to take because then it would not be your own but mine. Today you may have taken the wrong route, but the decision was yours. Had it been a success it would have been yours, too."

Drona argued, "Then why did you promise that you would guide me?"

The Guru replied, "I did. When you saw the footprints of the animals going in a different direction, it was a sign to follow. Don't you know animals go to the river to drink water? As you walked away from the footprints, didn't you see how the trees around you had dried up? I can only guide you through signs. If I had told you to not move forward, it would have been my decision, not yours. As for Nakul, he read the signs and that led him to the river."

"Does that answer your question, Madeline?" asked the Door. "Our universe exercises free will."

"I guess so, but what if like Drona, I don't understand the signs?" asked Madeline.

The Door smiled and replied, "You will learn."

"What if I don't?" questioned Madeline.

"You will grow," answered the Door.

STAY FIT, RELEASE THE PAIN

We take form so that our soul learns, heals, and grows. So, take care of your body in which you reside, for it is the temple of your soul.

While the Door stayed shut, Madeline found ways to exercise within the confines of her home. She would wake up early and follow a set workout regimen that would keep her energised throughout the day. Despite the daily workout she often complained of backache. To reduce the pain, she also included specific exercises for her back, but to her despair, nothing seemed to work.

One day when Madeline was exercising, she experienced an acute pain in her back that made her cry out in pain. Instead of resting, she continued to exercise.

The Door noticed this but did not say anything and let Madeline complete her workout. When she sat on the stool, exhausted, the Door said, "You should listen to your body."

Madeline replied, "If you are talking about the backache, there is nothing to worry about. It has been there for quite a while now and I have got used to it. Don't worry I am fine."

"If the backache persists, I suggest you consult a doctor on the phone," said the Door.

But Madeline ignored the suggestion and got on with her day.

 After a week Madeline once again complained of backache.

The Door reminded her, "Madeline, listen to your body."

Madeline snapped back, "You think I don't? I exercise every morning. I watch my diet. What else do you want me to do?"

The Door replied calmly, "The body remembers a lot, the mind sometimes figures things out later."

"What do you mean?" asked Madeline.

"If I say you look beautiful today, how will it make you feel?" asked the Door.

"It would make me feel good," replied Madeline.

The Door asked, "And what if I say that you are the worst person I have come across. How would that make you feel?"

"I won't like it. I will be angry, and I may say something harsh to you," answered Madeline.

"Does it end there?" asked the Door.

"Maybe…" said Madeline.

The Door replied sternly, "It doesn't. Whatever emotion you feel becomes a part of your soul and what the soul feels the body displays."

"So, you mean to say our every emotion has an effect on our body?" asked Madeline.

"Yes," replied the Door. "People often tell us to avoid, ignore, move on, and in the bargain, we repress the pain. We live as though nothing ever happened but what we fail to understand is that every pain, left unattended or suppressed can give rise to a physical ailment. Imagine that while playing you fall and experience immense pain in your leg. When you are taken to a doctor, you are informed that it is a fracture. If someone told you to ignore and move on, would you be able to do so?"

"Not at all," replied Madeline.

"But what if you ignore it?" asked the Door.

"That would result in dire consequences," replied Madeline.

"The same is with any kind of hurt we experience. It needs to be healed or else it will bleed into different areas of our life. Then one day it may appear in the form of a disease and while you would seek treatment, you may never be able to get to its core."

"So, what does it take to get to the core?" asked Madeline.

"Forgiveness," replied the Door. "You need to forgive yourself for the many times you caused yourself pain. You need to let go of what hurt you. If you hold on to hatred, envy, or even a grudge, it is baggage for your soul."

"How?" questioned Madeline.

"When you fight with someone, how long does it take for you to forget the incident?" asked the Door.

"Depends on what the fight was about," smiled Madeline.

"Something serious," said the Door.

"It would take me a month or two to forget the incident," replied Madeline.

"During this month or two, if someone mentions the person you had this fight with, how would it make you feel?" asked the Door.

"I would get angry and feel sad. It would remind me of the unpleasant incident," said Madeline.

"There you are," said the Door. "That feeling of anger and sadness is the burden you carry. Holding on to any bitterness means carrying a burden."

Madeline knew in her heart that she was carrying baggage, which she hid from everyone.

The Door continued, "Release it, Madeline. It doesn't serve you anymore."

Madeline was stunned. She stammered, "R-Release what?"

"The pain!" answered the Door.

Madeline confessed, "It's not that easy, you know."

"It's not that difficult either…" smiled the Door.

"What makes you so confident that this will heal my back pain?" asked Madeline.

"What doesn't control you has no power over you," said the Door.

HEALING

The wound must heal for the soul to be set free or it will hold it captive, for lifetimes to follow.

One night Madeline stayed up late reading a novel. After she finished reading few pages of the book, she took a deep breath and said, "Why does love have to be so tragic? Why can't it be simple?"

Toby raised his head and looked at her with sleepy eyes.

Madeline giggled, "No my boy, I am not talking about you. Your love is one of a kind." Then she took him in her arms and hugged him tightly. Toby snuggled up to her and fell asleep.

Madeline continued to read as the night grew cold. Occasionally she stopped and stared into space as if soaking in what she had just read.

Tears trickled down her cheeks. She brushed them away and continued reading.

In her heart Madeline knew that the storm had passed but there were days when its memories crawled to the windows of her heart that was broken by the malicious wind. She said, "I can't release the pain no matter how much I try…"

The Door looked at her with compassion and replied, "Keep the book away. It is late and at this hour you should not feed your wounds."

Teary eyed, Madeline sniffled, "You are right, but I don't know how to heal, or like you said, release."

The Door replied, "Firstly, keep the book away and promise me you will read it only after you have healed. Words have power and strength, Madeline. We read with our minds, but the words are absorbed by the soul. Healing is a process, it takes time. But it will definitely release the pain."

"How?" asked Madeline.

The Door answered, "First, we need to understand why it is here. Every pain comes into our life for a purpose. We don't understand this while we are struggling to mend our broken hearts. But once the fight is over, we begin to see the silver lining."

"How will we ever know its purpose?" asked Madeline.

"We need to look within. Pain demands change, my dear, and it is vicious till it completes what it is here to do," said the Door.

Madeline wiped the tears from her eyes and asked, "Is it the same with the anguish that lies on the other side of you?"

"It would be a lie if I say it is not so," said the Door. "The magnitude with which things are unfolding on the other side reveals the demand for change not just from outside but also from within. And I am afraid…"

"Afraid of what?" exclaimed Madeline.

"The destruction it will bring," replied the Door.

Wrapping a blanket around herself Madeline said, "Why does there have to be destruction for change to happen?"

The Door answered "It doesn't happen suddenly. The universe always sends us signs, but we tend to ignore them. That is when the Universe leaves us with no choice but to change our old ways. We grow through cycles of pain and healing. Through pain comes healing."

"All I see is suffering. Where is the healing?" asked Madeline.

"Healing happens in silence, while we are still fighting the pain. The sparrows have returned, you have had sightings of rare birds, you have heard of dolphins swim nearer to the shore, the air is cleaner, healing is happening."

"Maybe even I will heal one day," said Madeline.

"You were always meant to heal," replied the Door.

Madeline smiled and said, "That's comforting, but what should I do when memories cloud my mind?"

"Breathe," answered the Door.

"What good will that do?" asked Madeline.

"It will remind you of your soul that's reaching out to hold you," replied the Door.

KARMA

Travellers we are beyond time and space, carrying our deeds in the pockets of our soul, each lifetime an adventure to reap what we sow.

It was a Saturday afternoon, and Madeline was playing fetch with Toby, her dog, in the living room. After the game, both sat on the floor under the fan. Madeline gazed around and happened to notice the peephole on the Door. She said "Can I look through the peephole? I would like to have a glimpse of the other side."

The Door answered, "You won't be looking into a peephole. You would be looking into a circle."

Madeline looked puzzled. "A circle?" she exclaimed.

"Yes, where it all started," commented the Door.

Madeline walked to the Door and looked through the peephole. At first, it appeared dark and foggy, but it started to clear up. At a distance, she saw a pair of lion cubs playing, when a huge truck bounced off the mud road and approached them. The lioness was not around. Taking advantage of this, a man got down from the truck, grabbed the two cubs, and drove away. "Where are they taking the cubs?" whispered Madeline.

The Door stayed silent.

The scene changed and she saw the man put the cubs into a cage.

The scene changed again. She saw water and a huge fishing vessel. The men on board cast a fishing net into the sea. The pull was so hard that it rocked the boat. The men knew it was a huge catch. While the creature tried to escape it was dragged into the vessel and killed. "Why am I seeing such atrocities?" cried out Madeline.

The scene changed. This time she saw two children who barely had anything to eat, beg for food.

Madeline could not take it anymore. She moved away from the Door and wiped the sweat off her forehead. She said, "What was all that about?"

The Door replied, "Did you have any questions in your mind while looking through the circle?"

Thoughtfully, Madeline said, "I wanted to look at how the world is on the other side. I also wondered why mankind has to be locked behind Doors."

The Door replied, "Then what you saw was your answer."

"What do you mean?" asked a puzzled Madeline.

"When you looked through the peephole, you were looking into the circle of Karma. The peephole showed you why mankind is locked behind Doors. Why humans are being locked behind Doors was answered by the circle."

Madeline shrugged saying, "I was never a part of any of this. So why me?"

The Door explained softly, "We are all connected. In the universe, Karma works on different levels. In this case, it is collective Karma that has brought the world to a standstill. Human beings have exploited the earth and have claimed the right to show their might and power over land and sea. While the earth has endured, the universe must stand by the law."

"Is the Universe punishing us?" asked Madeline.

The Door replied, "Karma is never a punishment, it is a gift. Each one of us is here to learn and fill gaps in our soul so that we can grow. We are just travellers here on earth. The world was there before we were born, and the world will go on even when we cease to exist. So, all we can do is make the best of the lessons we learn."

Madeline pondered for a while, and then asked, "Can we change our Karma?"

The Door replied, "Everything is in our hands. We call the shots. The result of which becomes our Karma."

"But I don't understand, where do I start?" exclaimed Madeline.

"In the Now," replied the Door.

THE TREASURE OF GIVING

Make the act of giving an act of love so that when what you have given culminates, love will continue to linger in their hearts.

After hearing of what was happening on the other side of the Door, Madeline wondered if she could do something to help. She went to the Door. "I want to support people out there but if you keep me locked in, how will I do that?"

The Door said, "Let me tell you a story."

There once lived a rich man in a village, who was very renowned. One day he happened to take a walk in the nearby forest and spotted a monk meditating under a tree. The monk had a divine glow and a peaceful calm on his face. Seeing his heavenly aura, the rich man invited him to the village. He knew that if he did so, he would win the admiration of the village folks.

While the monk was deep in his meditation, the rich man decided to wait for him to finish. When the monk opened his eyes, he politely greeted the rich man and asked, "What brings you to the forest?" The rich man told him that he was taking a walk and came upon the monk. He invited him to the village for a feast. The monk agreed on one condition: that the village present him with something invaluable.

In the village, everyone prepared for the monk's arrival. They gathered around the village gram panchayat tree with various gifts. The monk settled under the tree, and the rich man introduced him to the villagers. The monk addressed them with a short speech. They presented him with flowers, pots, spices, grains, etc. Among the villagers, there was a child who was watching the monk accept various gifts from the villagers. He too wanted to gift something to the monk. After some thought, he ran home poured a glass of water into a small earthen pot and went to present it to the monk. When his turn arrived, he handed the monk a glass of water. The monk smiled and drank the water but said nothing. It was now time for the rich man to gift the monk something. The rich man reached out into his bag and presented the monk a precious stone – a ruby.

The monk asked, "Is this ruby mine from now?"

The rich man exclaimed, "Yes!"

"So, I can give it to anyone I like?" said the monk.

The villagers looked puzzled. The rich man nodded.

The monk gave the ruby to the boy who had given him water.

The villagers were stunned. They began to whisper among themselves. "For a glass of water, the monk is giving him a ruby!"

The rich man asked the monk why he had given the ruby to the boy.

The monk replied, "Because he deserved it."

The rich man was confused. "What do you mean? You asked us to give you an invaluable gift and you presented the gift to the boy?"

The monk smiled and said, "What could be more valuable than water when you are thirsty?" He folded his hands and said, "I am grateful to everyone for presenting me with beautiful gifts. While all of you were engaged in presenting your gifts, no one realised that I might be thirsty. This boy here noticed that I was getting tired and offered me a glass of water. What can be more valuable to a thirsty man than water?"

This explanation silenced everyone.

"Very often we miss out on small things that can add value to someone's life. I know your heart is clean and you want to go out there and make a difference, but you can do it right here," the Door said.

Madeline looked around the house and said, "Who will I be able to help within these four walls?"

The Door replied, "Don't tame the love that is in your heart. Let it run free, and it will show you where it is needed."

Madeline's phone rang. It was her friend Ruth. She did not sound good. After chatting for more than an hour Madeline hung up and returned to speak to the Door.

"Things are not good outside. People are losing their jobs. Minds seem to be in the most traumatic state," said Madeline. "It's good that Ruth reached out to me. I will try and do something for her."

The Door smiled, "Wasn't it you who said an hour ago that you can't help anyone by being within four walls?"

Madeline spluttered, "Well she is a friend…"

The Door said, "It doesn't matter whether you are helping a friend or a stranger. Today you are the reason someone knows that they are not alone. What is kindness if you neglect your near and dear ones and run out to comfort the world?"

Madeline knew what the Door was talking about.

The Door continued, "The world is going through turbulent times. The healthcare workers, police, governments are trying their best to get the situation under control. If they are advising us to stay at home, then why not help by heeding to instructions?"

Madeline asked, "Will this effort ever make a difference to the world?"

The Door replied, "It definitely will, and we will play a part in its healing."

EMOTIONAL DIET

Fill your soul with words, music, and conversations that trigger your pure spirit, for what you consume is what will dwell within you.

Madeline had just got done with work and settled in with a hot cup of coffee and some homemade Indian snacks to watch a good movie. She turned on the television but could not make up her mind. What would be that perfect movie? She asked, "Any suggestions on which movie is worth watching?"

The Door replied, "Watch a movie that you won't mind being a part of if it were true."

"Well, that didn't make it any easier to choose," said Madeline.

"Maybe, but that's the amount of mindfulness you need to have while selecting a movie," said the Door.

"It's just a movie. How does it even matter?" asked Madeline.

And the Door said, "Everything you watch, listen and speak becomes a part of you. You connect with it."

"How can it become a part of me? I am only watching it, and I know for a fact that it is not real," reasoned Madeline.

"What if I prove it to you?" challenged the Door.

Madeline smirked, "Well, then I will be more mindful of what I am watching."

The Door replied, "Very well, why do you cry when there is an emotional scene in a movie?"

Madeline began to stammer and her mind went blank. "Huh...what.. when did you see me cry while watching a movie?"

The Door laughed. "Couple of times."

"Well, that's me! Not everyone cries while watching a movie," Madeline protested.

"Not everyone cries but everyone definitely goes through a range of emotions while watching a movie," argued the Door. "Take a horror movie for instance. Don't you begin to feel scared even though you know your mind is tricking you? The mind is like a sponge absorbing everything that is around. Feed it love, positivity, and inspiration. For what you feed it is what it will digest."

Madeline took a sip of coffee and said, "How can we keep a check on everything our mind consumes?"

The Door replied, "Let me tell you a story."

Once a man took his grandson to a field. After they had walked for about ten minutes, they came to a fence with an oak tree in the middle. The man told the boy, how he, as a child, would come to the tree and play in its shade. The little boy was captivated by the beauty of the huge tree and began to visit the field often. Over time, the oak tree and the boy became best friends. The boy would spend hours sitting on its branches, playing under its shade, and speaking to the tree.

One day the boy decided to invite his friends from school to play beneath the tree. He told them how wonderful the tree had been to him and how he loved its company. All of them spent the afternoon under the shade of the tree. The next day when the boy went to school, one of his friends told him that he didn't like the oak tree. He found it rather creepy. The boy tried convincing his friend that it was not true, but the friend wouldn't listen. To prove his friend wrong, he went about asking his other friends about the oak tree. Everyone had a different opinion. Some said they loved it, some felt it was too old while a few mentioned that its branches were too slippery. After hearing what everyone had to say, the boy began to wonder if it were true. The more he thought about it, the more he began to see the tree in the same light as his friends.

He didn't know why he felt this way but he was going to stay away from the tree. He decided to visit the tree one last time to say a final goodbye. Gathering all his strength he walked through the field to where the oak tree stood. The oak tree asked him why he looked so sad and pale. The boy couldn't hold it within himself any longer and told the oak tree what his friends had said. He told the oak tree that he had come to say goodbye. The oak tree stayed calm and asked the boy if he could do one last thing before leaving.

The boy seemed hesitant at first but agreed.

The oak tree said, "I want you to bring two of your most trusted friends to spend a day under my shade."

The following Sunday he came with two of his most trusted friends to spend the day with the tree. The three of them enjoyed the cool breeze, the sound of rustling branches as they shared their picnic lunch. One of the friends said, "We should do this often, it's beautiful here!" The other continued by saying, "I feel we should make this our hideout and build our tree house here. It's simply perfect!"

Before leaving, the boy went to the oak tree and said, "We will come again tomorrow."

The oak tree smiled and said, "I always knew it wouldn't be a goodbye."

The boy felt embarrassed for what he had said earlier and asked the oak tree, how it knew that he wouldn't go away forever. The oak tree looked towards the setting sun and as it was getting late asked the boy to meet him the next day. That night the boy could not sleep as he was waiting eagerly for the sun to rise so that he could visit the oak tree again.

At break of dawn, the boy walked into the field where the oak tree stood. "Here I am, for the answer you promised."

The oak tree said, "When I asked you to return with only two good friends you knew exactly who they were. You could identify them by the way they support you, inspire you, the happiness they bring, the love they share, and above all the peace you feel when they are around. I knew they would be true to you. I knew that with those two friends, you would not only see my truth but also your own."

The Door continued, "Mindfulness is the key. Always be aware of what you are reading, watching, or conversing about. You need to choose who enters the boundaries of your mind. The boy initially invited everyone and due to their varied opinions, he would have lost the best companion he had. Our mind is like the oak tree but we need to decide who we let in."

Madeline took a sip of coffee and said, "What about those opinions that are already dwelling within us?"

"Like dry leaves, they will fall, when you don't pay attention to them," the Door said.

Madeline asked, "How long do we need to keep a check on who is entering the fence?"

The Door replied, as long as you want to stay connected with the oak tree which is the centre of your being.

FINDING YOURSELF

Your uniqueness fills a void in the universe, which only you could make whole. That's how precious you are and let no one make you believe otherwise.

There were times when Madeline looked back and let a silent tear roll down her cheek when she thought of memories now lingering in time. She had a faraway gaze in her eyes even though she was looking into the mirror as she combed her hair. To draw her consciousness back to the present, the Door shouted, "The fence is left open."

This jolted Madeline to the present. "When you love someone, you want it to last forever but suddenly, they choose to drift away and pretend to be strangers. What then?"

The Door replied, "You can be a friend to the one who needs you the most."

"Who would that be?" asked Madeline.

"That would be your own self," said the Door.

"It's easier said than done. When you are hurting, it is difficult to love yourself," said Madeline.

"Yet it is the best thing you will ever do for yourself," answered the Door.

Madeline lowered her gaze and thought.

The Door said, "Do you love yourself?"

"I am trying to," she said.

"Well then," said the Door "Consider this to be the right time. In solitude you begin to see the light within yourself."

"What is it like to love yourself?" Madeline asked.

The Door replied, "Self-love is building a relationship with yourself. This begins with acceptance. It is like falling in love with someone. When you are in love you spend time with them, you do things that make them happy. As days go by, you want the best for them, you protect and value them. You let no one disrespect them. That's the relation you need to have with yourself. We know how to love. What we need is to focus that love onto ourselves."

"Isn't that selfish?" asked Madeline.

The Door replied, "You see that basket there in the corner? Can you get it here?"

Madeline got up and dragged the basket near the Door. "What do you want me to do with it?"

"I need you to put a few things in the basket for me."

Madeline looked puzzled.

The Door continued, "Put in a bottle of brown paint, a brush, a white cloth, a gallon of water and some nails."

Madeline brought what the Door had asked for and put it in the basket.

The Door said, "I would also need some polish, turpentine, a chisel, and sandpaper."

Madeline looked at the Door and said, "We don't have it at home. Can you open so that I can go out and get it?"

"Nice try!" the Door chuckled. "You will find it if you look for it."

To convince the Door she looked around but returned empty-handed. "If I don't have it, how will I be able to give it to you?" grumbled Madeline.

The Door smiled, "So is it with love. You need to first have it before you give it to others. When we don't love ourselves enough, we search for someone who can fill that void. If that person is unable to do so, we find faults in that person. So isn't it best you feel complete first rather than look for that someone to complete you? Now would you still call it self-love or being selfish?"

Madeline thought about it and said, "I guess, I have a long way to go…"

The Door replied, "You always knew how to love. You need to know how to love yourself the same way."

"Any tips for this journey?" asked Madeline.

"Be kind to yourself, even on days when nothing seems right. Remember the way you treat yourself, is the way the world will learn to treat you."

REACHING WITHIN

We continue to live on. Our lifetime is an opportunity to learn, grow and heal. Remember why you are here and stay close to your purpose.

Madeline was restless after being at home for close to a year. She stared at the Door and ranted, "How much longer! It's not easy you know. Tomorrow is my birthday, and I am stuck at home. This is not the birthday I imagined."

The Door understood but there was nothing that it could do. "Even though I would love to see you go out, I am forced to keep you in here for your own safety."

"It's my birthday!" exclaimed Madeline.

The Door answered calmly, "I know how you feel but maybe this time your birthday is meant to be celebrated differently. And it may be a birthday you will remember for a lifetime."

"I sure will," huffed Madeline.

"It's not that bad to be at home, Madeline. You are surrounded by people you love. Your family is in good health. Trust me, it is a blessing in such times. You have the privilege to blow those birthday candles and make any wish you please. For many, all they wish for is to see another day, to spend time with their loved ones, just one last time."

"You are right," said Madeline. She walked to the window and took a deep breath. "How can I make this birthday special, then?"

The Door sensed the calmness in her tone. "Your birthday will always be special, Madeline, whether you celebrate it or not."

"How is that?" asked Madeline.

The Door replied, "The universe thought that you were needed on earth and that you would fit into its plan so gracefully while finding your very own path."

Madeline asked innocently, "Why do you think we come on earth?"

The Door explained, "We come on earth to evolve. Our soul needs to learn to love, to forgive, to heal, and to make whole, of what was left incomplete. That's why we must accept the challenges that come our way. For they are here not to punish us, but to reveal what we need to learn."

"So, this means what's happening now is a part of the universal plan?" asked Madeline.

"Yes," admitted the Door. "You and I are part of the mosaic."

"Around the world, so many people are leaving us," grieved Madeline. "How will we ever be able to accept that it was all a part of a higher plan?"

The Door answered, "No one really leaves us, Madeline. The soul is eternal and continues to live on. All we can do is send them love and peace."

"Will we ever meet them again?" asked Madeline.

The Door comforted Madeline saying, "It's only one lifetime, my dear."

These words made Madeline feel hopeful and she looked towards the Door with great admiration. "So, on a lighter note," said Madeline "What will you be getting me for my birthday?"

The Door laughed. "That's a surprise! Don't be impatient."

The next morning Madeline woke up to birthday wishes from her family, phone calls from friends, and texts messages on her phone. She was overjoyed and glided around the house happily.

The Door called out to her. "Madeline, can you sit with me for a while?"

She quickly approached the Door and before the Door could even wish her, she asked, "Can I have my gift now?"

The Door smiled. "Happy Birthday, Madeline. Here is your gift." The Door gave her a little box which was gift wrapped with a blue ribbon.

Madeline could barely wait to open it. She gently untied the ribbon and opened the box. On a velvet cushion, was a small key. She took the key in her hand and asked, "And which door does this open?"

The Door cackled, "I was waiting for you to ask me."

"Well then, tell me."

The Door replied, "If you hold this key in front of any Door, it will open and you can walk through it."

"This little key has a lot of power," said Madeline in surprise.

"It does and it must be used wisely," warned the Door.

The key sparkled with sunlight bouncing off its golden edges. She placed it back into the box and put the box in the cupboard.

"That's a gift to remember. Thank you," said Madeline.

"With the power of choice..." added the Door.

FINDING DIVINITY

At the core of our soul lies the light of our creator, serene and all-knowing. Yet we look around when the truth is within.

Madeline was done with her work for the day and was sitting at the window watching the glorious hues of orange and pink of the setting sun. Her phone rang. It was Nirav who sounded very tense. Their friend Rupi was in the hospital. Madeline was shocked to hear this. She had spoken to Rupi a week back and she had seemed perfectly fine. How uncertain life could be. She was upset that she couldn't meet Rupi because the Door held her in.

She sighed, "Is it all destiny? Is there nothing we can do?"

The Door said, "When there is nothing we can do, it's time to close your eyes and connect with the One."

"If everything is destined, how will my prayers help?" asked Madeline.

The Door replied, "You are right when you say everything is destined. But if there is anything that can alter destiny, it is grace."

"Grace!" exclaimed Madeline. "How does grace change destiny?"

The Door replied, "Before I explain that to you, I want you to pray for your friend's speedy recovery."

Madeline went to her room to pray. "I am all ears. Tell me how grace alters destiny," she said on her return.

The Door asked, "What is destiny?"

Madeline thought for a while and said, "What is bound to happen."

"Why are certain events destined in our life?" questioned the Door.

"I remember you telling me, certain events appear in our lives to teach us a lesson," replied Madeline.

The Door agreed, "Yes, sometimes the way learning transpires is difficult, and the soul must endure much suffering. When we pray, we ask for divine intervention and it is through grace that we receive the strength, support, and knowledge we need to overcome a situation. There are also times when divine intervention forces events to change their course completely to support us. And that is what we call a miracle."

"Why don't miracles happen often?" asked Madeline innocently.

"Miracles do happen every moment, Madeline, but they are different from the miracles we desire," replied the Door.

Madeline drew a deep breath, "I just want Rupi to return home safely." Her phone rang. It was Nirav again. Rupi's condition had worsened. She was shifted to the ICU. Hearing this, Madeline began to panic. "How could her condition have worsened?" exclaimed Madeline.

The Door who was watching her said, "Don't worry, at this moment you need to radiate positivity. You can't let fear get the better of you." While the Door tried its best to put Madeline's worries to rest, nothing seemed to calm her.

Madeline kept pacing to and fro in the hall. "What does it take for a miracle to happen?" she asked the Door.

"Faith," replied the Door.

THE TEMPTATION

Be mindful, for temptation disguises itself as the most beautiful lie and lures free will to take its side.

Rupi's condition improved, and soon, she was out of the ICU. Madeline kept herself up-to-date on her progress. After ten days, Rupi called up. Madeline was almost in tears when she heard Rupi's voice over the phone, but she tried to hide them. They spoke for more than an hour that day.

After hanging up the phone, Madeline went to the window and sat there quietly, looking outside. A thought ran through her mind, "Why don't I do something exciting? Something that I haven't done in a long time!" She remembered the key the Door had gifted her on her birthday. A mischievous thought occurred to her. Why not use the key on the Door, who gave it to her in the first place and who restricted her from going out. She approached the Door very cautiously and said, "You remember the key you gave me? I want to use it," she said with a challenging look in her eyes.

The Door suspected it wouldn't like what was to follow. It asked, "So which Door would you like to open?"

Madeline, a bit reluctantly, asked, "Would you open and let me out?" There was sudden silence.

The Door, diffused the uncomfortable silence and asked Madeline, "Are you sure this is what you want?"

Madeline replied, "Yes, it's been a long time. Maybe this is how it's destined to be."

The Door agreed. After ten months of staying firmly shut, it opened. Madeline was excited to step out. She thanked the Door, but got no reply.

Outside the building, she took a deep breath as if inhaling all the air around her. She walked to the park and strolled barefoot on the grass. She felt content and like a little child, she found happiness in watching everything happening around her - the greenery, people, and the soft scent of the flowers. When she returned, the Door allowed her in, but stayed silent. In her excitement Madeline didn't notice. The next day she used the key to go out again. This continued for a week. During this time, the Door barely spoke to her.

One day, on her way to the park, a man approached her to ask for directions. As she was directing him to his destination, he sneezed. Madeline took a step back in alarm. The man thanked her and went on his way.

When Madeline came home, the Door let her in but did not say a word. Sipping on tea, Madeline asked, "Are you angry with me?"

The Door replied, "No, I am just worried."

"Worried! About what?" exclaimed Madeline.

"The coming days seem dark. People have begun to lower their guard. They feel the battle is over, but it is too early to claim victory."

Madeline asked, "What could possibly go wrong?"

The Door replied, "I hope nothing does."

Later that night, Madeline complained of a mild headache. At first, she thought that it was due to the new outings every day. But she was alarmed when she developed a fever. She raced to her mother's room. "Mom, I have a fever," she said. Her mother checked her temperature. The thermometer read hundred.

Seeing the situation, the Door said, "Madeline, don't allow anyone near you."

"Have I caught the virus?" she asked in a quavering voice.

Door answered, "I am afraid you have. Ask everyone to maintain distance from you."

Madeline obeyed and instructed her family to act accordingly. Her father called the doctor, who prescribed some medicines and a test to be conducted the next morning. That night was a terrifying one for Madeline. She sat alone in her room, angry with herself for being careless.

She couldn't speak to the Door as she had to stay in her room. She regretted asking the Door to let her out. She also remembered everything that the Door had taught her and decided that she wouldn't let negative thoughts destroy her. She calmed her mind and decided to get the test done the next day. With the medicines prescribed by the Doctor, her temperature subsided but she chose to quarantine herself in her room till the test results came in. Whenever she peeped out of her room, she would see her parents trying to hide their worry. Toby, her puppy lingered outside her room waiting for the hug that he always got from Madeline. She could see her brother making arrangements in case things worsened. In her heart, she felt terribly guilty.

Her mother gave her food in disposable cutlery. That evening when she was served tea, there was an envelope with a letter in it, on the tray. She quickly opened the envelope. It was a letter from her parents.

Dear Madeline,

As a child whenever you were upset you would lock yourself in your room. Your Dad and I used to get very worried in the beginning, but then explained to ourselves that, if this helped you get over matters, we should let it be. Today to see you lock yourself in the room makes us anxious, but at the same time, we know you are only trying to protect us. We want you to know that we are proud of you and no matter what the results show we will overcome it together.

Madeline, don't be harsh on yourself. If God forbid, you test positive, you need all the energy to fight the virus, and any sort of resentment will only make you weak.

While every minute waiting for the results may seem like waiting forever, we want you to always think of God and pray to him.

You are a strong woman, Madeline. Don't let the situation get the better of you.

Lastly, we want you to know that we love you. Dad, Chris, Toby, and I are right outside if you need anything.

Take care, love always.

Madeline had tears in her eyes, but she decided she would be anything but weak.

When the results were in, Madeline tested positive.

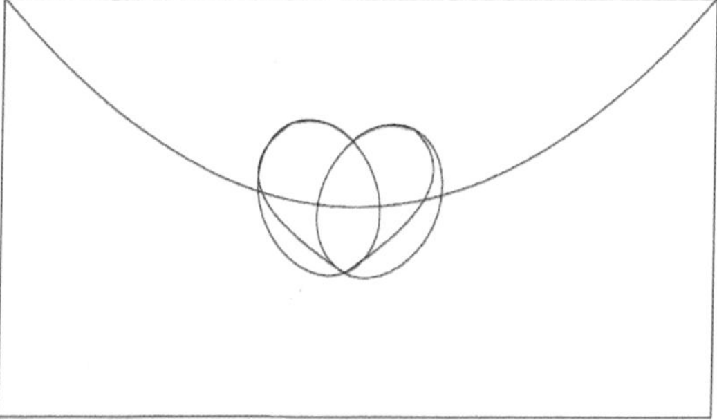

THE APOCALYPSE

It will catch you off guard and your strength will be determined by what you hold within. The fury of destruction is such that it will tear down everything that needs to be re-built. It may seem like the lash of a thousand canes and may leave a gaping hole in your heart. No one said the apocalypse would be forgiving.

According to the rules for fighting the disease, the other members of the family were also tested. Madeline maintained mental and emotional stability and was responsible about taking the prescribed medications. When the test results of her family members came in, all of them were tested negative, to their immense relief.

While Madeline was glad to hear this, she knew the fight against the virus had just begun. If she had to heal herself completely, she had to follow the medication schedule and other instructions very diligently. Quarantine was not easy. There were nights when she woke up tired and restless and wished for her mom to be by her side.

Her mom provided her with nutritious and tasty food but Madeline had lost her sense of taste. But she forced herself to have her meals. She inhaled hot steam three times a day and kept a tab on her oxygen levels.

Maybe the virus was here to teach her to learn to take care of herself and her health. After struggling with the disease for nearly a week, she realised that she also had to keep her mind alert. Like the Door would say, "Keep an eye on who you allow within the fence."

On days when she regretted her haste in using in key, she would replace these thoughts with positive ones. She thought of all the love, care, and good wishes her family and friends showered on her. On the ninth day, Madeline's oxygen level dropped. She panicked but knew that the virus had to be fought with the mind as much with the body. So she did exactly as the doctor instructed her.

It took a month for the test results to come back as negative. She had won the battle. Her family members exchange smiles with tear filled eyes. But Madeline continued in isolation for another week.

A week later, on a Sunday, the family decided that it was time for celebration. Madeline's mother decided to cook some of her best dishes.

That day they sat around the table with grateful hearts and every morsel was a blessing. From the corner of her eye, Madeline could see her mother beaming with joy. After lunch, everyone settled in for an afternoon nap.

Madeline stayed back. She had not spoken to the Door since she tested positive. She was too embarrassed to start a conversation. The Door stayed silent, too. Finally she said, "You were right when you refused to let us out. I know, I took advantage of the key that you gave me on my birthday. I used it against you and I am extremely sorry. I now understand you were only trying to protect us. Won't you ever speak to me again?"

The Door asked, "How is your health now?"

Madeline replied with a smile, "I am fine now. I practiced everything that you taught me when I was locked up in my room. And that is why I am fine."

The Door replied, "Everything happens for a reason, but it has passed now and what matters the most is that you are safe." The Door continued in a grave voice. "Be at home for as long as I don't let you out. The second wave of the virus is here, and it is going to be even more devastating."

Madeline was terrified. "A second wave?" she exclaimed. "But hasn't a vaccine been developed?"

"Yes," replied the Door. "But it is not available for everyone. You don't need to worry as long as you are at home...

"I won't repeat my mistake again," assured Madeline.

Days passed and around the month of March when everyone was convinced that life was getting back to normal, the virus began its invasion again. It walked among crowds and spread the seeds of death. The cries of the apocalypse were worse than before. Hospitals were overflowing with patients and people stood in serpentine queues at the crematorium. Madeline dreaded every phone call.

The Door stayed shut. The other side was dark and dreadful. Madeline asked the Door, "Why is there a second wave?"

"The night is always darkest before the dawn," said the Door.

A NEW WORLD

It is time to start again. This time more mindful about life and the planet, with an understanding that we are a part of a greater whole and love binds as well as heals us.

The second wave continued to be brutal and unforgiving. It didn't spare anyone. Madeline stayed at home and never asked the Door if she could venture out. She enjoyed quality time with her family, continued to work from home, focused on her health and stayed connected to her friends through audio and video calls.

She would look out of the window at the beautiful sights of nature - birds, squirrels, trees, and the ever-changing dramatic sky. One day she asked the Door, "Where are we heading from here?"

The Door replied, "We are in the making of a new world."

Madeline asked, "There is so much suffering and destruction everywhere. Is this what the new world is about?"

The Door replied, "Like a seed, we are buried under the soil now. While it may all seem unreasonable, a time will come when we will clearly understand its purpose." A few sparrows appeared at the window and began to hop from one clothesline to the other. "You see those little sparrows. Just a few years back they were close to extinction. Look at them today. They have returned. Nature has a way of healing itself. Maybe this was needed, maybe human beings had to learn this lesson the difficult way."

Madeline nodded.

The second wave continued creating havoc, but the vaccine to combat the virus was finally announced to be available for adults. This was a ray of hope. Madeline informed the Door about the latest development.

The Door said, "The time is near."

"Time for what?" asked Madeline.

"For Doors to open again," it replied.

Hearing these golden words, Madeline felt a thrill of anticipation. "I wonder how this new world will be."

The Door replied, "Exactly as you want it to be."

"What do you mean?" asked Madeline.

The Door answered, "The new world will build itself on our thoughts, actions, and the love we spread in the world."

"You are right. I guess it's time to say goodbye to the old world and embrace the new. So is there anything you want me to carry, as I move forward into the new world?" asked Madeline.

"Always remember the lessons from the old world," said the Door.

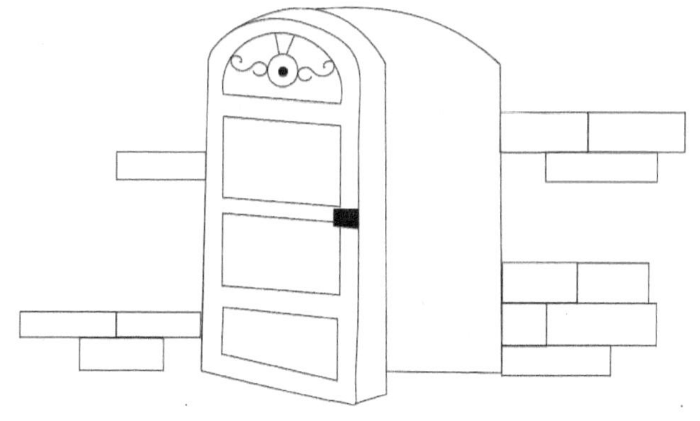

ACKNOWLEDGEMENTS

I owe my sincere gratitude to God who has inspired and guided me in writing this story.

Followed by my Mom and Dad who have been extremely supportive and optimistic towards my every goal.

A heartfelt thanks to Horatious, my brother, for believing in me and being my rock, my best friend, and my strongest critic.

Also, would like to thank my friends and colleagues for their great support and faith in my endeavours. To Anchal Agarwal for taking the time out to provide editorial advice during the first draft of the book.

A special thanks to the Publishing house Become Shakespeare.com for guiding me in publishing my first book. Ms. Miral Bheda for her professionalism and pace as a coordinator. The designer Diraj Navlakhe for putting together a beautiful cover and finally timely advice and editorial insights by Sita Bhaskar, Editor at Become Shakespeare.com

This book was possible because all of you believed in me.

Thank you

ABOUT THE AUTHOR

Martina Pinto is a Marketing Communication Manager and a self-taught visual artist. She resides in Mumbai, India with her parents and her younger brother. Martina pursues business writing as a part of her work profile. She also shares a profound passion for painting and photography. Martina has always believed in the power of positivity and inner strength, which she depicts in everything she does.

Martina loves to write poetry, some of which have been published in local journals. She has also contributed a story that was published in the novel Her Voice - Finding Yourself.

Martina likes to travel and pen down learning's from her escapades. She is very fond of animals and loves to stay in tune with nature, as she believes that it strengthens the human spirit

www.ingramcontent.com/pod-product-compliance
Lightning Source LLC
La Vergne TN
LVHW091715190726
843493LV00001B/310